Communication Skills

NIPA® GENX ELECTRONIC RESOURCES & SOLUTIONS P. LTD.
New Delhi-110 034

About the Authors

V. L. V. Kameswari is the Professor and Head, Department of Agricultural Communication at G.B. Pant University of Agriculture and Technology, Pantnagar, Uttarakhand. She completed her M.A. in Communication from the University of Hyderabad and Ph.D. in Journalism & Mass Communication from Makhanlal Chaturvedi National University of Journalism and Mass Communication. She has over 30 years of teaching experience at UG and PG levels. She started her career as Lecturer in the Faculty of Communication at IIFM, Bhopal and has taught courses related to communication skills, media production and development communication. She was Fulbright Scholar-in-Residence at the University of Fort Smith, Arkansas, USA.

Arpita Sharma Kandpal is Assistant Professor in the Department of Agricultural Communication, College of Agriculture, GBPUA&T, Pantnagar. Earlier, she was Assistant Professor in the Directorate of Extension Education, Anand Agriculture University, Gujarat. She obtained her M.Sc. and Ph.D. degrees from the Department of Agricultural Communication, College of Agriculture, GBPUA&T, Pantnagar. She got class merit scholarship during her school period, Teaching Assistantship during M.Sc. and UGC-JRF Fellowship in Ph.D. She also received ICSSR Post Doctoral Fellowship. She has cleared ICAR as well as UGC NET. She got best poster, best oral as well as young scientist award in different conferences.

Amardeep is Professor (Agricultural Communication) in G.B. Pant University of Agriculture and Technology, Pantnagar in Uttarakhand. Having doctorate degree in Development Communication, he has expertise in educational technology and media. As an academician he has vast experience of around 23 years in teaching Undergraduate, Master's and Ph.D. courses along with design and restructuring of many courses related to communication, extension education, educational technology and media. So far, he has guided 11 Doctoral and 19 Masters theses researches. He has published one book, four edited books, nine book chapters in book, 45 research papers in reputed journals and more than 50 popular articles.

Communication Skills

Volume 3 The Protocol Series

V. L.V. Kameswari
Professor and Head
Department of Agricultural Communication
G.B. Pant University of Agriculture and Technology
Pantnagar, Uttarakhand

Arpita Sharma Kandpal
Assistant Professor
Department of Agricultural Communication,
College of Agriculture
G.B. Pant University of Agriculture and Technology
Pantnagar, Uttarakhand

Amardeep
Professor
Department of Agricultural Communication,
College of Agriculture
G.B. Pant University of Agriculture and Technology
Pantnagar, Uttarakhand

NIPA® GENX ELECTRONIC RESOURCES & SOLUTIONS P. LTD.
New Delhi-110 034

NIPA® GENX ELECTRONIC
RESOURCES & SOLUTIONS P. LTD.
101,103, Vikas Surya Plaza, CU Block
L.S.C. Market, Pitam Pura, New Delhi-110 034
Ph : +91-11-43860225, Mob.: +91 9717133558, 9540816132
E-mail: newindiapublishingagency@gmail.com
Website: www.nipaersources.com

Print ISBN: 978-93-58877-11-3
ebook ISBN: 978-93-58878-60-8

NIPA® also publishes books in a variety of electronic formats. Some content that appears in print may not be available in electronic books, and vice versa.

Composed and Designed by NIPA®.

Preface

Communication is fundamental to human existence. We are engaged in the process of communication throughout our lives – either overtly or covertly. However, our understanding of the process is very limited and people often equate it with good oratory. The scope of communication goes way beyond speaking effectively and encompasses situations ranging from speaking in front of a large gathering to musings when we are alone. In today's world, effective communication skills are essential for success at workplace. Breakdown of interpersonal relationships, conflicts at workplace and dismal electoral performances all have one thing in common – communication failure.

The New Education Policy-2020 has revamped the education system with the intention of making the country's youth future ready. Keeping in line with the NEP – 2020, the ICAR has also restructured undergraduate education in agriculture and allied disciplines. Under the new structure, some courses will be offered to students of agriculture and allied disciplines as common courses. These common courses have been deemed important as they deal with skills vital for developing all round personality and success at work place.

Communication Skills is one of the common courses under the NEP – 2020. The course covers topics ranging from interpersonal communication to handling mass media. This practical manual contains twenty five activities pertaining to various topics covered in the course on "Communication Skills". Activities given in this manual will help the students gain a better understanding of communication process at interpersonal, group and mass levels and impart skills necessary in various walks of life. It will help them communicate more effectively and confidently. This book will be useful to faculty members, students and trainers associated with developing better communication skills.

Authors

Contents

1

To Get Acquainted with Classmates

Date:

Objective: To get acquainted with classmates.

Description: This is the first lab activity and has been designed to make the students feel comfortable in their new surroundings. The aim is also to help them get acquainted with their classmates as they are still new to each other. This short fun activity will help them mingle and set the tone for upcoming activities.

Activity: Make two piles of chits. One pile (A) should have name of the country and the other contains name of their capital city (B). Divide the class into two groups. Ask one group of students to pick up one chit from pile A randomly. Ask the other group to do the same from pile B. Now, ask students have to search for their partner (country/ capital). Once, the entire class has found their respective partners, ask one from each pair to gather information about their partner. After 5 minutes, the other person will ask questions to know about the partner. At the end of the session, call each pair and ask them to briefly introduce their friend.

Observations:

Teacher's Signature & Date

2

To Understand Communication Process and Its Elements

Date:

Objective: To understand communication process and its elements.

Description: Communication is the process by which a person shares knowledge, feelings, ideas, and information, etc. with another person(s) in such a way that each gains a common understanding about the meaning and intent of the message. Major functions of communication include sharing information, issuing instructions, persuasion and motivation. There are several elements in communication process. Anyone who takes the initiative and starts the communication process is called the source or communicator. The intended recipient of the communication content is called as the receiver. Any sign or symbol which has the same meaning for the source and the receiver is called is the message. Receiver is the intended recipient of the message and what the communicator hopes to accomplish is the objective of communication process. The medium through which the message moves from the source to the receiver is called as the channel. In any communication process, it is important that the message sent by the source is clear, and understandable. This can only be ensured when the receiver responds to the message in the form of feedback. Feedback can be defined as the message from the receiver to the sender that indicates the receivers understanding or agreement. Feedback is source oriented, varies according to the communication situation, affects the source and exerts influence over future communication process. Audience response is change in behaviour, understanding or knowledge and/ or attitude. Quite often, it is observed that certain factors prevent a message from getting through to the intended audience or disrupt the communication process. These are known as barriers to communication.

Activity: Divide the class into pairs and make them sit back to back. Give a line drawing to one person (A) and a blank sheet and pencil to the other (B). In the initial 5 minutes, A can only describe the drawing and B has to draw it on the blank page. At the end of 5 minutes take away the sheet from B and give another blank paper. Repeat the activity, but in round 2, B can ask questions or seek clarifications. At the end of the activity give the sheets back and ask the pairs to compare the two drawing and discuss the process. How many pairs got it right the first time? Which drawing was more accurate – first or second? Why was the first drawing more distorted?

Observations:

Teacher's Signature & Date

3

To Understand the Significance of Non-Verbal Communication

Date:

Objective: To understand the significance of non-verbal communication.

Description: Non verbal communication refers to communication without the use of words. It can encompass a wide range of communication behaviour from body language to choice and use of architectural objects. It is used for repeating, substituting, complementing, regulating verbal messages and deceiving. Some of the common non verbal means of communication include:

Gestures: Gestures are movement of body parts and kinesics refers to the study of body movement.

Posture: It refers to the degree of erectness of the body and can reflect state of health, profession, etc.

Body orientation: The degree to which a person faces towards or away from another person during communication. It conveys relationship between two or more people, status, etc.

Paralanguage: Paralanguage refers to nonverbal aspects of speech and includes tone, pitch, speed of delivery, etc.

Eye contact: Eye contact may be defined as the extent of visual engagement with another person. It can be used to convey power, confidence and emotions.

Touch: Tactilics refers to the use of touch to convey message. Touch can be friendly or hostile.

Time: Chronemics is the study of use of time in non-verbal communication. How much time is given to another person indicates importance and attitude towards that person.

Space: Proxemics refers to the study of use of space in nonverbal communication. People carry an invisible space bubble around them which expands or shrinks according to the situation and relationship with people. Space between people can be divided into intimate, personal, social and public distance.

Facial expressions: Face is the most visible and prominent part of the body. Facial expressions can be used to convey a range of emotions. Facial expressions are also the most deceptive of nonverbal behaviour as we learn to control our expressions from a very young age.

Besides these, clothing, architecture, objects, choice of colours, etc can also convey messages nonverbally. It is important to remember that nonverbal communication is culture and context specific and can only be understood along with verbal messages.

Activity: Make two piles of chits. One pile (A) contains names of body parts and the other (B) contains the name of an expression. Invite students/ volunteers and ask them to pick up one chit from each pile. Each of them has to convey the expression/ feeling picked up by them only using the body part mentioned in the other chit. Ask the rest of the class to guess the expression/ feeling. Note down how many get it right. Why were others not able to do it correctly? Did they find it easy or difficult to express themselves nonverbally? Which feelings or expressions were difficult to convey nonverbally?

Observations:

Teacher's Signature & Date

4

To Understand the Importance of Paralanguage in Verbal Communication

Date:

Objective: To understand the importance of paralanguage in verbal communication.

Description: Paralanguage is the variation in voice and includes vocal characteristics such as pitch, range, resonance, tempo, etc. Though it is an integral part of verbal communication, it is quite distinct from the actual signs and symbols that are used by the communicator. For example; people generally lower their voice towards the end of a statement, but raise it towards the end if they are asking a question. Paralanguage can reveal the speaker's age, emotional state, personality, etc.

Activity: Divide the class into pairs. Ask each pair to select a sender and a receiver. Distribute the activity sheet given in the box (Activity Sheet 1) to all the pairs. The sender has to repeat the statement written in the activity sheet emphasising the word written in bold each time. Ask the receiver to write the meaning derived every time a different word is emphasised. Does the meaning change when a different word is emphasised by the speaker? What is the meaning of the statement in each case?

Activity Sheet 1

<u>Anil</u> didn't say that you are dumb.

Meaning : ______________________________

____

Anil **<u>didn't</u>** say that you are dumb.

Meaning : ______________________________

____

Anil didn't **<u>say</u>** that you are dumb.

Meaning : ______________________________

____

Anil didn't say that **<u>you</u>** are dumb.

Meaning : ______________________________

____

Anil didn't say that you are **<u>dumb</u>**.

Meaning : ______________________________

____

Observations:

____

____

____

____

____

____

____

____

Teacher's Signature & Date

5

To Practice Giving Appropriate Feedback

Date:

Objective: To practice giving appropriate feedback.

Description: Communication is a cyclic process. The message originates from the source and is reaches the receiver. The receiver then decodes the message (i.e; makes sense)and sends a message back to the sender to convey his/her understanding or agreement with the message that has been received. Feedback not only completes the communication cycle, but also takes the process forward. Without feedback from the receiver, communication process will come to an end. Feedback has several functions in communication process:

a) Evaluation of the message: Feedback tells the sender how well the message has been understood by the receiver and whether the message is up to the desired level. For example; when a student receives a feedback on his/ her class presentation, it tells how well they have performed.

b) Initiate change: Feedback also helps in bringing about a change in the sender or the message. In the above example, if the feedback says that the presenter is not making eye contact with the audience, the student can make a deliberate effort to look at the audience during the presentation.

c) Reinforcement: Feedback can be positive or negative. Consequently, it can reinforce or deter certain behaviour. For example; words of praise by the parent for good academic performance can spur the child to do even better next time. On the other hand, reprimand by the teacher for talking in the class may deter the student from repeating the same behaviour.

Hence, it is important to learn to give effective feedback. There are six different feedback styles.

a) Judgemental: In this type of feedback, the receiver makes a judgement about the message, as well as the sender, by implying that the sender is at fault.

b) Directive: Feedback of this nature tells the speaker what to do or offers advice.

c) Empathetic: Empathetic feedback gives emotional support to the sender. In this case, the receiver tries to convey compassion and understanding towards the sender.

d) Questioning: As the name indicates, this type of feedback probes the sender to reveal further information. But, the receiver may or may not be supportive towards the sender.

e) Interpreting: In this case, the receiver tries to help the sender understand the situation better by offering alternate explanation or asking questions.

f) Active: Active feedback involves conveying the receiver's willingness to listen. This is done by asking supportive questions and paraphrasing.

Activity: Distribute a copy of the activity sheet given below (Activity sheet 2) to all the students. Ask them to provide different types of feedback to the statement written at the top of the sheet. Invite them to read out their feedback one by one. Which style is the best? Why?

Activity Sheet 2

Rajat: I lost my brand new iphone yesterday.

Judgemental : ____________________

____

Directive : ____________________

____

Empathetic : ____________________

____

Questioning: ____________________

____

Interpreting : ____________________

____

Active: ____________________

____

Observations:

____

____

Teacher's Signature & Date

6

To Understand the Concept of Perception and Its Role in Communication

Date:

Objective: To understand the concept of perception and its role in communication.

Description: Human body receives stimuli through various sensory organs and the brain processes these stimuli and assigns meanings leading to a reaction. This process of organizing, identifying and interpreting of sensory stimuli leading to an understanding of the environment is called perception. During the communication process, the human body receives stimuli through the ears (in case of verbal communication) or eyes (in case of written communication) and the impulses are transmitted to the brain. The sounds or words are interpreted leading to a response and the communication process takes place. Though the human body is constantly being bombarded by stimuli, it does not respond to all of them. A significant portion of the stimuli from the environment is screened out and only what is deemed important is processed. This screening out of some stimuli is known as selective perception. Selective perception occurs at three levels – cognitive, emotional and physiological. Due to selective perception, the same situation may be interpreted differently by different people. Hence, perception plays an important role in communication.

Activity: Ask the students to keep their notebooks and pens aside. Display the activity sheet given below (Activity Sheet 3) and tell the class to take a look at the sheet. Display the activity sheet for 2 minutes and close it. Now ask the students to write down all the words they are able to recollect. What is the maximum number of words remembered by the students? What is the minimum number? Were there any words which were remembered by most of them? Did these words have any specific features?

ACTIVITY SHEET 3

Hello ***United States of America*** Olympics **leg** **July** come

day Donut Rushmore ~~**Niagara**~~ Lakshmi

Uttarakhand ***Go*** *large* **Dosa** Dean **Calendar**

Pen phone owl ***chair*** Bus *Do* **Book** cricket **New**

Zealand notice

Rajyalakshmi **pot** *welcome* Rajasthani **Lucknow**

Spoon bread **elephant** **fox** wolf ***table***

Nagpur ***Sania Mirza*** Pakistan

Switzerland ~~**Jammu**~~ Japan Tokyo Textbook **Bag**

Gucci Lakme Mouse Flower **Perth** **Dudley**

Washington Shanti ~~**Madhuri**~~ *Mamta* India

College *Bat*

Observations:

Teacher's Signature & Date

7

To Understand Gap in Communication Process

Date:

Objective: To understand gap in communication process.

Description: Communication is never 100 percent efficient. In other words, even an ideal situation does not lead to complete and full understanding between the sender and receiver. Often, the receiver may understand the message differently or receive only a part of the message. This happens as every individual has a different frame of reference. Frame of reference is the set of experiences, beliefs and values which influence a person's behaviour and acts as a benchmark against which all new stimuli are interpreted. Based on the frame of reference, every individual develops a perception. Perception is the process of receiving and interpreting stimuli. Perception not only differs from person to person but is also selective. Communication gap refers to the disparity between the message sent by the sender and the way it has been received. While some degree of distortion is inevitable, large gap will lead to breakdown of the communication process. Communication gap occurs if the message does not reach the intended audience at all or is received partially or does not have the intended effect. Communication gap can be reduced by repeating the message, taking feedback, giving complete information on time.

Activity: Divide the class into groups comprising of 7-10 students. Ask each group to select a sender. Once the sender has been identified, ask rest of the members to stand one behind the other at touching distance. Sender has to stand at the end of the line with other members in front of him/ her. Show a simple line drawing to the sender only and ask the student to convey the line drawing (message) to the person in the front. The sender can only draw the figure on the person's back and group members are not allowed to speak. The second person has to convey the message further to the person in the front in a similar manner and the process goes on. The last person in the sequence (i.e the person in the front), however, has to draw it on a paper. Repeat the exercise with all the groups and then show the original drawing. How does the original figure compare with the figure drawn by the group members? Is it similar? Which group was most accurate and why? Which group showed maximum distortion? Why?

Observations:

Teacher's Signature & Date

8

To Understand the Characteristics and Limitations of Language

Date:

Objective: To understand the characteristics and limitations of language.

Description: Language is the structured system of symbols, which are called as words. Semantics refers to the study of the relationship between symbols and their meaning. All languages are arbitrary as the word symbol is not the thing it represents (i.e. if all of us agree, we can refer to a "cat" as "donkey", without turning it into one!). Words can be both abstract (things that cannot be sensed directly) and concrete (things that can be experienced through sensory organs). Language is also vague and ambiguous. Lastly, words can have both denotative (factual/ objective meaning) and connotative (subjective/ psychological) meaning.

Activity: Give a copy of the activity sheet (Activity sheet 4) to all the students. Tell them to rewrite the sentences by replacing the underlined word. After the activity has been completed, ask the students to form pairs and exchange the activity sheet with their partner. How many pairs rewrote the sentences in the same/similar manner? Which sentences were most difficult to rewrite and why? How many statements did they rewrite differently? Do both the partners feel that what the other person has written is also correct? What characteristics of language were highlighted in this activity?

ACTIVITY SHEET 4

a) I visited Ooty during the summer break.

b) I love my mother.

c) I lost my phone.

d) She misses her brother.

e) There is a hibiscus tree in front of my house.

f) Rose garden is very large.

g) Inaugural ceremony of the Paris Olympics was organised on Seine river.

h) Today is Teachers' Day.

i) Yoga is good for health.

j) He stood up to receive the award.

Observations:

Teacher's Signature & Date

9

To Prepare a Non-Projected Audio Visual Aid (Chart)

Date:

Objective: To prepare a non-projected audio-visual aid (chart).

Description: Audio visual aids are media that can make communication more effective through use of sound and visuals. They are of two types – projected and non-projected aids. Non projected aids are visual materials that are used as it is by the instructor and do not need any device or equipment. Examples include charts, posters, leaflets, flash cards, etc. They are easy to prepare, carry and use. They can be prepared as and when needed and multiplied at low cost. Due to these advantages, non-projected aids are frequently used in instructional settings.

Chart is a commonly used non projected audio-visual aid. Chart is a thick sheet of paper containing information in a summarized form. It can be used to convey a large amount of information in an interesting and effective manner. It can be used for showing trends, comparison and similarities, besides linkages between various sub-components. Here are some simple tips for preparing effective charts:

a) The chart should be kept simple.

b) Confine it to a single idea or message.

c) Arrange content in a sequence.

d) Use colours (2-3 only) to explain and differentiate the content.

e) Use lines and bars in only one dimension.

f) Give an appropriate title.

g) Leave adequate margins on all sides.

Activity: Divide the class into groups comprising of 2-3 members. Ask them to choose a topic and prepare a chart. After everyone has completed the task, ask each group to make a short presentation using the chart they have prepared. Give feedback to the students.

Observations:

Teacher's Signature & Date

10

To Prepare a Non-Projected Audio-Visual Aid (Folder)

Date:

Objective: To prepare a non-projected audio-visual aid (folder).

Description: Folder is a single thick sheet of paper, which is usually folded once or twice. Folder contains essential information about a place, event, etc. which is printed on a good quality paper. A folder is prepared as and when needed and is distributed free of cost. Here are some useful tips for preparing a folder:

a) Make it interesting and attractive.
b) Insert graphics, illustrations and photos related to the main theme.
c) Avoid using white background.
d) While folders are usually half or tri-folds, one can try unique folds, sizes and shapes.
e) It should have an eye-catching and appropriate title.
f) Insert event or organization's logo.
g) Include complete address and contact details of the organization/ person.

Activity: Divide the class into groups comprising of three members. Ask them to decide on a topic and prepare a folder. After everyone has completed the task, ask each group to make a small presentation about the folder they have prepared.

Observations:

Teacher's Signature & Date

11

To Prepare a Non-Projected Audio Visual Aid (Poster)

Date:

Objective: To prepare a non-projected audio visual aid (poster).

Description: Poster is a placard displayed in a public place to raise awareness. A well-made poster must attract attention of passers-by and motivate them to take action. Here are a few tips for making effective posters:

a) A good poster should rely on pictures rather than words. While there is no strict rule regarding the number of words, try to use no more than 10-12 words.

b) The font size should be big enough to read from a distance as posters are displayed at public places. If there is a variation in font size, increase the size as you move from top to bottom. In addition, while choosing colours, keep the background against which the poster will be displayed in mind.

c) Use contrasting and attractive colours. This will help in drawing the attention of the viewers. However, the colours or their combination must not be jarring.

d) Most common size of poster is 18x24, 24x36 and 27x40 inches. Decide the appropriate size based on the background and location of the poster. If it is going to be put up in large public places like an auditorium or subways, use a large size.

e) Pre-test the poster before finalizing it. Modify the message, layout, design, etc. if needed, before making the final version.

f) The poster should have one pictorial element that becomes the focus of viewers' attention. Rely on close-up shots, striking colours, contrast, unique design, etc. to direct viewers' attention.

g) Avoid using several small pictures.

h) It is essential that a poster has some blank or empty space positioned in a creative manner. While it is not essential to leave set margins on all sides, avoid filling up the space end to end with visual elements or words, unless it adds to the overall visual appeal.

i) The goal of a poster is to create awareness and motivate people to act. Hence, always include an action point for the readers. Be definitive about what you want them "to do".

j) Use good quality paper/ material for printing the poster. One can also experiment with different printing techniques and unique styles to enhance the appeal.

k) Keep the theme and audience in mind while designing the poster.

Activity: Divide the class into groups comprising of three members. Ask them to decide on a topic and prepare a poster. After everyone has completed the task, ask the students to display their posters. Request a colleague to evaluate/ give feedback.

Observations:

Teacher's Signature & Date

12

To Prepare a Projected Audio-Visual Aid (Power Point Presentation)

Date:

Objective: To prepare a projected audio-visual aid (power point presentation).

Description: Audio-visual aids that are magnified and projected on to a screen are called as projected audio-visual aids. There are three methods of projection:

a) Direct projection: In this case, light rays from the source of illumination pass through condenser lens, then hit the object and go through objective lens and fall on the screen. Slide projector is an example of direct projection.

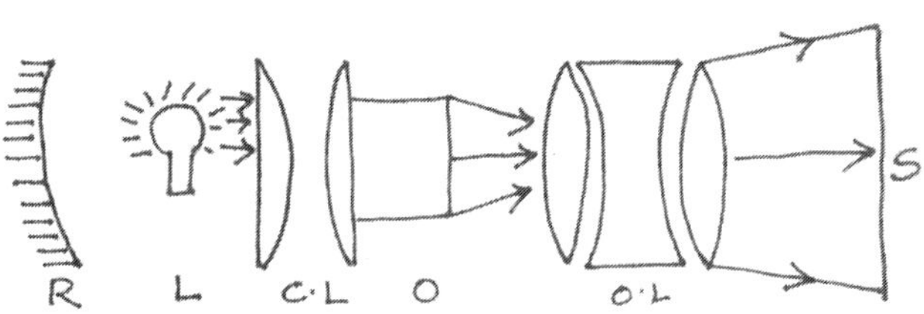

Figure 1: Direct Projection

b) Indirect projection: Light rays from projection lamp enter one half of the condenser lens and are reflected on to a plane mirror placed at 45°angle to both axis of the lens. Light rays then pass through the other half of the lens and enter the object. After passing through the object, they are reflected by another plane mirror placed at 45°angle before being projected on a screen. Example of indirect projection: Over Head Projector.

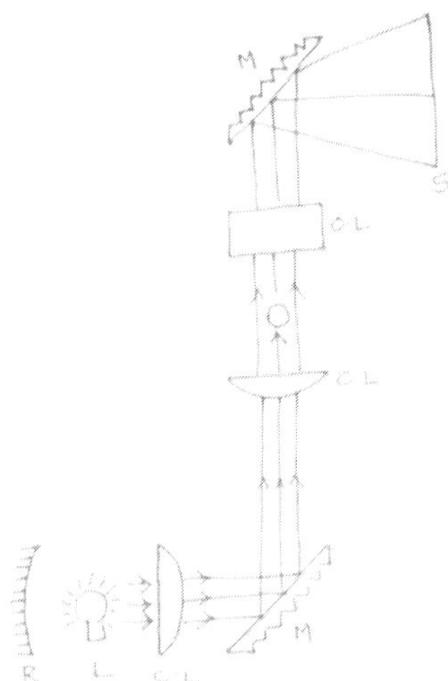

Figure 2: Indirect Projection

c) Reflected projection: In case of reflected projection, light from the lamp or source of illumination hits the object at an angle and reflected image is captured by a mirror, which is placed at 45°angle. The image then passes through the objective lens before being projected on a screen. Epidiascope is an example of reflected projection.

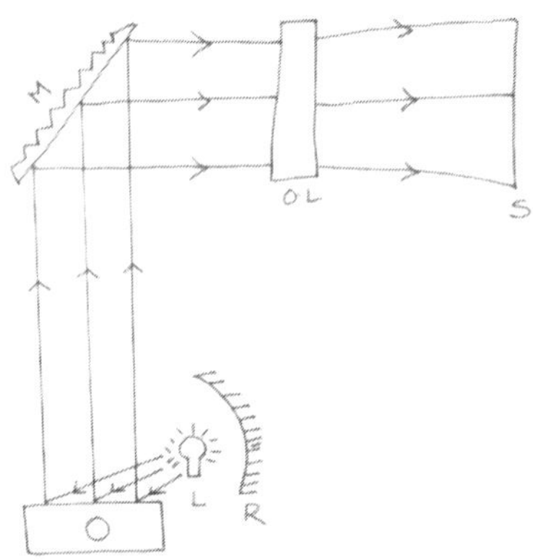

Figure 3: Reflected Projection

Power Point is a presentation software designed by Microsoft. It is commonly referred to as PPT and is used to create dynamic slideshows on computer. Power point presentations can incorporate figures, animation, photos, videos, and sound, making them very effective. Power point presentations are only used to make better presentations and should not be used as a stand-alone medium. Here are some tips to make effective power point presentations.

a) Use a single background throughout the presentation.
b) Choose a font size and type that is visible to everyone in the room.
c) Use bullet points instead of running text.
d) Use only key words or write in brief. Avoid long and verbose sentences.
e) Do not clutter the slides.
f) Use other visual elements (charts, figures, photos, animation, etc.) wherever possible.
g) Give a short and relevant title to each slide.
h) Arrange content in a proper sequence and use hyperlink for additional information.

Activity: Divide the class into pairs. Ask them to decide on a topic and prepare a brief power point presentation. Ask each group to make a brief presentation on the chosen topic using the power point presentation. Ask other students to evaluate the presentation.

Observations:

Teacher's Signature & Date

13

To Practice Group Discussion and Understand the Do's and Don'ts of Group Discussion Process

Date:

Objective: To practice group discussion and understand the do's and don'ts of group discussion process.

Overview: Group discussion is a form of discourse, which occurs when more than two people recognize a common problem, exchange and evaluate information and ideas. Their efforts may be directed towards a better understanding of the topic or solving a problem. Group discussion occurs in a face-to-face or co-acting situation. It is a democratic method in which equal opportunity is given to every participant to express his/ her opinion. In formal settings, group discussion takes place under the direction of leader. Group discussion is often used by academic institutions or employers to assess certain traits and skills of the participants. The number of participants usually is around eight, but there is no hard and fast rule. When being used as a method of assessment/ evaluation, the group is given a topic. The participants are allowed a few minutes to understand the topic and organise their thoughts. Then the topic is open for discussion among the participants for about 20 to 30 minutes. Group discussions are of three types: topic based, case-based and task based (often called group task). In topic- based group discussion, the participants are given a topic by the evaluators. This topic can be controversial (e.g Should euthanasia be legalised in India?), abstract (e.g; 0) or factual or informative (e.g. Agro climatic zones of India)

Activity: Divide the class into groups comprising of 6-8 students. Assign a different topic to each group and give them 30 minutes (5 for preparation+ 20 for discussion+ 5 for conclusion). Ask another group to act as evaluators and observe the following competencies and give the feedback.

Team work: How did the group members work together? Were they supporting each other? Were they giving others an opportunity to express themselves?

Communication skills: Did the team members have good communication skills? What kind of negative or positive body language were they using? What kind of feedback did they give others?

Influencing: Which group members were able to influence others? What strategy did they use?

Managing conflict: Were there any conflicts within the group? Did it effect the outcome? How was the conflict resolved?

Observations:

Teacher's Signature & Date

14

To Practice Case-Based Group Discussion

Date:

Objective: To practice case-based group discussion.

Overview: A case is a detailed description of anything that has happened in real life. In a case, real names are often changed to ensure confidentiality and protect the privacy, but it is not a fictitious account. A case presents a situation, or a problem and the learner is expected to suggest a solution based on the information given in the case. Case based group discussion is often used to test the analytical and reasoning ability of the participants. While participating in a case-based group discussion, the students should start by recognising and defining the problem. This is followed by listing as many solutions as possible with contributions from all the group members. In the next step, each solution is evaluated critically by the group members keeping in mind the information/ data/ facts given in the case. Finally, the best possible solution is put forth by the group. It is important to remember that there are no right or wrong solution as any option is often a trade-off.

Activity: Divide the class into groups comprising of 6-8 students. Assign a different case to each group and give them 30 minutes for discussion (5 for preparation+ 25 for analysis). Give feedback on the following points:

Was the group able to identify the problem / issue? Did the participants generate a variety of solutions? Did everyone contribute to idea generation and problem solving? How did the group arrive at the solution?

Activity Sheet 5

Case: Pill-age

Ipill or intelligent pill is a highly effective emergency contraceptive manufactured by Cipla, an Indian pharmaceutical company. The contraceptive, which is a hormonal pill, is targeted at married women to prevent unwanted pregnancies when other 'regular' methods may have been missed by the couple. Doctors recommend the use of iPill only in case of emergencies as its frequent and/or regular use can lead to ovarian damage and menstrual problems, especially among younger women. Though its sustained and long term use can be dangerous, ipill is an over-the-counter (OTC) product and hence, can be purchased from the medical stores without a doctor's recommendation/prescription. About three months after iPill was introduced into the market, it was found that a number of teenagers were approaching the medial stores for the pill. Most of them reported using it as a regular contraceptive pill to be "doubly safe" following an increased teenage sexual activity in recent years. Medial shop owners in the national capital report that the demand for iPill is more in affluent areas of the city.

Observations:

Teacher's Signature & Date

15

To Practice Group Task

Date:

Objective: To practice group task.

Overview: Teamwork and good interpersonal relationships are of great importance in professional life. Hence, organizations often use various methods to test qualities such as communication/influencing/leadership skills. One commonly used method is assigning group task to the candidates. Group task requires striking a balance between team goals and individual success. The team members are expected to contribute to the overall goals while furthering their individual objectives. Additionally, the evaluator can observe leadership skills, team spirit, communication skills, analytical and decision-making skills of the group members without being intrusive. One can also judge the role for which a particular member is best suited. The time assigned for a task-based group discussion/ group task can range from 10 to 60 minutes depending upon the complexity of the task.

Activity: Divide the class into groups comprising of 6-8 students. Assign the same task to all the groups but ensure that the students do not mingle across the groups while performing the task. Assign the time depending upon the task. Make sure that all the materials required to complete the task are available to all the groups. After the allotted time is over, check how many groups have completed the task before providing the answer. Invite each group to discuss their experience around the following questions:

Did you accomplish the task? Why/ Why not? How did you go about the task? Who generated the ideas? Who among the team members did the actual task? Was there any conflict within the group? What role did each member play? How did the group arrive at the solution?

Activity Sheet 6

"Bahubali Construction Ltd."

Divide the class into groups comprising of 5-6 students. Each group has to construct the tallest, strongest and most beautiful tower using the material provided. Set up a shop selling newspapers, colour sheets, scissors, stapler, staples. Each group can pick up only four items from the shop to construct the tower. Give the students 30-45 minutes to complete the activity. Compare the towers on the basis of all three criteria and award the "Best Tower" prize to the group. You can make the task more complex by putting a price tag on the items in the shop and giving each group some money to start the "construction work".

Observations:

Teacher's Signature & Date

16

To Make Group Presentation

Date:

Objective: To make group presentation.

Description: Group presentation refers to presentation of subject matter by few or a group of people. Group presentations are fairly common in professional life and hence, one should have a mastery over how to prepare and make group presentations. If handled properly, group presentations have several advantages over individual presentations. They are more attention grabbing and interesting as the mere presence of more than one individual introduces variety into the process. Work can be shared among the team members and knowledge and resources can be pooled for better outcome. However, group presentations can also present several challenges and following points should be kept in mind for effective group presentations:

a) Divide the tasks based on expertise, interest and personality traits of group members.

b) Assemble the content into a cohesive presentation rather than using a piecemeal approach.

c) Maintain uniformity in presentation, style, physical appearance, etc.

d) Meet regularly during the preparatory phase to know what others are doing and to build a collective narrative.

e) Agree upon who will perform some of the key functions (such as operating the AV aids, introduction, handling questions, etc.) before hand.

f) Decide on the physical positioning of the members in advance.

g) Practice as a group before the actual day of presentation.

Activity: Divide the class into groups comprising of 3-4 members. Either assign a topic to each group or give a broad area from which they can choose their topic. Give the groups some time to prepare and arrange for presentations on a pre-decided date and time. Evaluate the presentations and provide feedback to the groups.

Evaluation Form				
S. No.	**Criteria**	**Performance**		
		Satisfactory	**Needs improvement**	**Unsatisfactory**
1	Clarity of purpose			
2	Organization of content			
3	Presentation style			
4	Pronunciation, speed and voice projection			
5	Use of AV aids			
6	Non verbal behaviour			
7	Ability to answer questions			
Additional comments:				

Observations:

Teacher's Signature & Date

17

To Practice Public Speaking

Date:

Objective: To practice public speaking.

Description: Public speaking refers to communication with a large number of audience in a face-to-face situation. Public speaking differs from most other types of communication as the roles of sender and receiver are distinct and different. Also, in case of public speaking, the onus of taking the interaction forward primarily lies with the speaker. Consequently, many people find it daunting and stressful and try to avoid public speaking situations. However, everyone can become a good public speakers with a little planning and practice. Following steps can be used for delivering an effective public speech:

a) Selecting the general purpose: This refers to the overall goal of the speech. Main purpose of the speech can be giving **information**, **persuading** listeners to your point of view or simply **entertaining**. While there can be some overlap, it is advisable to prepare and deliver the speech with one primary purpose.

b) Select a topic: While selecting a topic keep the general purpose in mind and ensure that it can be adequately covered in the given time. Also, choose a topic that is appropriate and interesting for your audience. Lastly, the audience should not be overly familiar with the topic.

c) Write the goal statement: This is especially important in case of informative speeches. It specifies, what you want your audience to learn or know at the end of the speech.

d) Analyze your audience: Knowing the characteristics of the audience is important for effective public speaking. Understand the demographic characteristics of your audience and what they already know about the topic. It will help in choosing the appropriate content and presenting new information to the audience.

e) Research: Gather as much information as possible about the topic from various sources. Ensure that the sources of information are credible and cross check the information. Sources can include books, journals, experts, etc.

f) Organize your speech: After assembling the content of the speech, arrange it properly. Speech can be organised on the basis of time, space, topical, comparison and contrast. In case of an informative speech, ensure that the speech is arranged into an introduction, body and conclusion.

g) Prepare supporting material: Supporting material can include various types of audio visual aids such as power point presentation, chart, folder, leaflet, photographs, etc. They should be prepared well in advance and in adequate number to be effective. In case you are planning to use projected AV aids, make arrangements for the equipment and ensure that they are working properly.

h) Practice: Practice make a person perfect, so rehearse your speech before delivery. This can be done by recording it and reviewing or requesting a friend to provide a feedback. Rehearsing is important, especially if you are a novice. But do not memorize your speech as it will sound very stilted. Use reference cards for recall, prompting and smooth delivery.

i) Delivery: Public speech can be delivered in four ways i.e. impromptu (speaking without preparation), manuscript (reading from a written text), memorized (memorizing the speech before delivery) and extemporaneous (using key words and phrases to take the speech forward). Try to follow the extemporaneous style. Pay attention to pronunciation, articulation, speech, pitch and voice modulation while delivering the speech.

Activity: Ask each student to choose a topic and prepare a five minutes speech. When they are ready, ask each one of them to deliver the speech in front of the class and provide feedback. You can do a video recording of the speech and give it to the students to help them improve their public speaking skills.

Observations:

____

____

____

____

____

____

____

____

Teacher's Signature & Date

18

To Practice Giving An Entertainment or Special Occasion Speech

Date:

Objective: To practice giving an entertainment or special occasion speech.

Overview: Entertainment and/ or special occasion speeches are short, simple and often meant to be humorous and entertaining. Special occasion speeches include welcome address, award presentation/ acceptance speech, after dinner speech, farewell speech, eulogy, etc. Entertainment or special occasion speech is often an impromptu speech i.e. they are usually given without any preparation. Here are some thumb rules of delivering an effective entertainment or special occasion speech.

a) Jokes/ anecdotes should be appropriate for the occasion and audience.

b) Some speeches do not call for humour/ entertainment.

c) Have a main point/ theme of the speech.

d) Relate the speech to the occasion.

e) Collect your thoughts before starting the speech.

f) Keep the speech short and simple without repeating the content.

Activity: Ask each student to deliver an entertainment or special occasion speech in front of the class and give a feedback. Allot five minutes to each student. Topics may include:

a) Introduce yourself during the orientation program at the college.

b) Give a speech as the class representative at your school farewell event.

c) Give a speech at the retirement party of your colleague who is retiring after 30 years of service.

d) As an award winning biologist you have been asked to make a speech after the dinner at an international conference.

e) Your boss has been transferred to another branch. Give a speech at the farewell function.

f) Give a speech about a well respected teacher who has passed away.

g) As the Dean of the college welcome the new students.

h) You are being presented the "Student of the Year" award. Give an acceptance speech.

i) Deliver a speech as the Chief Guest at the inaugural ceremony of the Sports Day function.

j) Deliver a speech to fill in the gap between two programs during a cultural event.

k) Welcome a delegation of students from France who are visiting the University on a study tour.

Observations:

Teacher's Signature & Date

19

To Write a Radio Script for Infotainment Program

Date:

Objective: To write a radio script for infotainment program.

Overview: Radio is an electronic audio medium that can broadcast messages to a large number of dispersed audience. Radio has several advantages as a medium of communication, especially in rural areas:

a) Radio can be carried around.

b) Low cost of production and ownership.

c) Usage is not limited by literacy and technical know-how.

d) It can be used by the listener while doing other tasks.

e) Usage is not limited by power supply.

f) Easy to operate.

Radio programs can be of various types such as interview, talk, discussion, feature, magazine, documentary, drama, etc. Irrespective of the type, most programs require a script. Scrip is the blueprint of an audio-visual production and scriptwriting is the process of creating a narrative that usually tells a story.A script is used to communicate information about and to people involved in program production. Main objective of an audio-visual production can be to give information to the audience, entertain them, educate them or convince them to a particular viewpoint. An infotainment program provides information in an entertaining way. This strategy has the advantage of holding audience attention while conveying facts or information, which are usually overlooked by the audience.

Example of a Radio Script

[OPENING MUSIC]

Interviewer: "Good morning, I'm [Name] and today we have with us an eminent marine biologist. Dr [Name]. He and his team have recently discovered a new species in the Indian Ocean. Dr [Name] Welcome to the show. Can you tell our listeners about this new marine species?"

Dr [Name]: "Good morning, everyone. We discovered this new species quite by accident. Our team is still examining whether it is a new species, or an evolved version of species found in the area."

Interviewer: "What are the implications if it is an entirely new species."

Dr [Name]: "If it turns out to be a new species, it will pose a challenge to the present system of classification."

All radio programs involve the use of three sound elements – spoken word, music and sound effects. While writing a radio script, keep the following points in mind:

a) Give an appropriate and catchy title.
b) All directions, sound effects and music should be written in brackets and upper case.
c) The name of the character/ talent is written in bold and lower case.
d) Dialogue spoken by the character/ talent is written against their name in lower case.
e) All pages are numbered.
f) Avoid long sentences and words and lengthy numbers.
g) Radio script should be written for the ear.

Activity: Divide the class into groups comprising of three students. Ask each group to choose an important social issue. Each group must convey the message in an entertaining manner and ask them to write a script. If production facilities are available, the students can produce the programme after finalizing the script.

Observations:

____

____

____

____

Teacher's Signature & Date

20

To Understand Basics of Photography and Practice Taking Good Quality Photographs

Date:

Objective: To understand basics of photography and practice taking good quality photographs.

Overview: Photograph refers to any image which is created when light falls on a photosensitive surface. With the advent of mobile phones and decreasing cost of technology, many people are taking up photography as a hobby or profession. Photographs are very useful in communication, extension and education, as they arouse interest, simplify complex ideas/ things, can be used to convey messages to illiterate people, and enhance credibility of the information. Apart from technical expertise, it is important to know the basics of composition to take good photographs. These include:

a) The photograph should be balanced i.e. the four quadrants of the image should complement each other.
b) Use leading lines to direct viewer's attention to the main subject.
c) Use colours carefully and strategically as they can make or mar, the composition.
d) Use appropriate light and lens to create depth of field i.e. illusion of third dimension in the photograph.
e) Place important elements at the intersections following the rule of thirds.
f) Use positive and negative space appropriately to create mood and effect.
g) Provide some space between various elements in the photograph to avoid a cluttered look.
h) Distribute the visual weight across the photograph in a balanced manner.
i) Focus your camera on the main subject.
j) Learn the basics of ISO, shutter speed and aperture.

Activity: Ask each student to shoot and print three photographs (you can give themes). Arrange for display of all the photographs and provide a feedback.

Observations:

Teacher's Signature & Date

21

To Visit a Video Production Facility to Understand the Process and Set Up

Date:

Objective: To visit a video production facility to understand the process and set up.

Overview: Video programs are often produced in a studio environment as it is convenient, easy to manage and there are very few disruptions. A typical video production facility comprises of two areas – control room and the studio floor. Director, assistant director, video and audio technicians sit in the control room. The control room has a series of monitors that display the final and camera outputs. It may also have "on air" and "preview" monitors which display images being broadcast and to check the image before recording, respectively. The control room also has a production console, which is used to select the video and audio output.

Actual action takes place on the studio floor. It contains all the essential equipment required for production, such as, cameras, microphones, lights, etc. in addition to the set. The talent performs on the studio floor, which is recorded by the production crew.

Activity: Arrange a visit to the nearest video production facility. Provide the students with an opportunity to interact with the production team and observe video program production.

Observations:

____

____

____

____

____

____

Teacher's Signature & Date

22

To Understand Shot Sizes in a Video Production

Date:

Objective: To understand shot sizes in a video production.

Overview: Shot, in video production refers to one continuous recording by the camera. It comprises of a series of frames (still images) and There are 24 frames in one second. A shot includes eeverything recorded between switching on and switching off the record button on the camera. It can contain movement of both camera and talent. Following are the standard shot sizes:

a) Extreme long shot (ELS) - shows a broad view of the surroundings along with the character and coveys scale, distance, and geographic location.
b) Long shot (LS) - shows the entire character from head to toe.
c) Medium long shot (MLS) - shows a character usually cut off above or below the knees. It is wide enough to show the physical setting in which the action is taking place, yet it is close enough to show facial expression.
d) Medium shot (MS) - shows a character's upper-body, arms, and head.
e) Medium Close-up (MCU) – framed from top of the head to shoulders and is used for showing reaction/ emotions of the subject.
f) Close-up shot (CU) - shows a character's face. It is close enough to show subtle facial expressions clearly.
g) Extreme close-up shot (ECU) - shows only a part of the character's face. It fills the screen with the details of a subject.

Video production mostly uses MLS, MS and MCU due to small screen size. LS is used towards the beginning and end of the program.

Activity: Ask each student to choose a one-minute clip of any video program and list all the shots used sequentially with brief description.

Observations:

Teacher's Signature & Date

23

To Write a Script for a Short Video Production

Date:

Objective: To write a script for a short video production.

Overview: A script is a written document that contains description of the setting, characters, dialogue, and stage directions for an audio-visual production. It is used to communicate information about actors, costumes, sets, and other aspects of production to those who will be involved in program production. While screenplay tells a story, a script (especially shooting script) mainly helps in production. Another difference between a screenplay and a script is that the former conveys what the audience will see on the screen, whereas the script guides the production team. A storyboard refers to pictorial representation of shots in a sequential order. It is very handy during shooting short videos like commercial or public service messages. Lastly, treatment is the summary or synopsis of the production. A good script:

a) Takes into consideration the characteristics of the medium.

b) Grabs audience interest and attention.

c) Presents the idea within the limitations of personnel, time, budget, etc

d) Fulfills the primary objective of the program.

Video	**Audio**
1) Fade Up to a Two Shot of the Host and the Guest in the Studio	(FADE UP MUSIC)
2) MCU of the Host	(FADE MUSIC UNDER) HOST: Good morning, I'm [Name] and today we have with us an eminent marine biologist. Dr [Name]. He and his team have recently discovered a new species in the Indian Ocean. Dr [Name] welcome to the show. Can you tell our viewers about this new marine species.

3) MCU of the Dr. X	DR X: Good morning, everyone. We discovered this new species quite by accident. Our team is still examining whether it is a new species, or an evolved version of species found in the area.
4) MS of Host	HOST: What are the implications of your discovery, if it is an entirely new species.
5) MCU of Dr. X Zoom Out to a Two Shot.	DR X: If it turns out to be a new species, it will pose a challenge to the present system of classification.

A script usually includes shot size, sound elements, description of the set, camera movement, subject movement and action. Video program production usually uses a two-column script in which:

a) The page is divided into two columns.
b) Left hand side column is for describing the video.
c) Corresponding audio is written on the right-hand side.
d) All shots are numbered sequentially.
e) Dialogue is written in small letters and the character's name(s) appears in upper case letters.
f) Audio cues are written in caps in brackets.
g) Shot size and other directions are written in caps in brackets.
h) Description of action is aligned with the left margin of the page.
i) Shot transitions are written in upper case letters and aligned with the right margin.
j) The title page of the script should contain the name of the program, script writer's name, and contact information.
k) All pages of the script, except the title page, are numbered.

Activity: Divide the class into groups comprising of three students. Ask each group to write the script for a short video program (no more than 10 minutes). You may also specify the format and theme.

Observations:

____

____

Teacher's Signature & Date

24

To Write an Article for a Farm Publication

Date:

Objective: To write an article for a farm publication.

Description: Print media can be used at the receivers' convenience and can be preserved for future reference. It can also be used to reach the readers at a relatively low cost and the information can be verified by the reader. Due to these advantages, print media is an important form of communication, especially for development purpose. The term "farm publication" is used to refer to any publication that is prepared by an extension agency/ development department and contains information related to improvement of farming practices. Farm publications can be of various types such as leaflet, folder, magazine, newsletter, etc. Farm publications are very useful for literate farmers and can also be used by illiterate farmers with the help of others. Basic principles of writing for farmers and other rural readers include:

a) Use simple language by replacing technical terms with local or commonly used terms. Avoid use of abstract words and jargons.
b) Write short sentences and short paragraphs. Divide the content into several small paragraphs instead of writing a long essay.
c) Use clear, relevant and good quality pictures and photographs as they improve readability and comprehension.
d) Content should be timely and seasonal.
e) Divide the content into various sections and arrange them in a logical sequence.
f) Ensure accuracy of content.
g) Place the most important information at the beginning.
h) Give a catchy and relevant title that grabs readers' attention.

Activity: Divide the class into pairs and ask them to write an article keeping the above points in mind. Let the students choose the topic, but specify the word limit. Provide a feedback and ask them to revise the article, if needed.

Observations:

Teacher's Signature & Date

25

To Visit a Newspaper Organization to Understand Its Structure and Functions

Date:

Objective: To visit a newspaper organization to understand its structure and functions.

Description: A newspaper is a periodic publication containing written information about current events and other information that is of interest to the readers. A newspaper organization usually consists of the following departments:

a) Editorial department: The editorial department collects, processes and finalizes all content and images that are published in the newspaper. News/ information collected by the journalist or contributed by various writers is made readable, presentable and attractive to the readers through editing and proof reading by the editorial team.

b) Production department: The production department is responsible for the timely printing and publication of the newspaper. It is involved in composing, paste-up and printing of the newspaper.

c) Business department: This department looks after the circulation and sale of newspaper space i.e. advertising. It collects advertisements from various organizations and ensures steady flow of revenue to the newspaper. The circulation manager engages sales agents and hawkers at various places to ensure the timely delivery of the newspaper.

d) Human Resources department: The HR department manages the human resources employed by the organization and is responsible for remuneration, incentives, assessment, etc.

Activity: Arrange visit to a nearby newspaper. Take the students on a guided tour to various departments and provide an opportunity to interact with key personnel.

Observations:

Teacher's Signature & Date

Index